# Quick Study

Scott
Foresman

**Editorial Offices:** Glenview, Illinois • Parsippany, New Jersey • New York, New York
**Sales Offices:** Parsippany, New Jersey • Duluth, Georgia • Glenview, Illinois •
Coppell, Texas • Ontario, California

www.sfsocialstudies.com

## Program Authors

**Dr. Candy Dawson Boyd**
Professor, School of Education
Director of Reading Programs
St. Mary's College
Moraga, California

**Dr. Geneva Gay**
Professor of Education
University of Washington
Seattle, Washington

**Rita Geiger**
Director of Social Studies and
  Foreign Languages
Norman Public Schools
Norman, Oklahoma

**Dr. James B. Kracht**
Associate Dean for
  Undergraduate Programs
  and Teacher Education
College of Education
Texas A&M University
College Station, Texas

**Dr. Valerie Ooka Pang**
Professor of Teacher Education
San Diego State University
San Diego, California

**Dr. C. Frederick Risinger**
Director, Professional
  Development and Social
  Studies Education
Indiana University
Bloomington, Indiana

**Sara Miranda Sanchez**
Elementary and Early
  Childhood Curriculum
  Coordinator
Albuquerque Public Schools
Albuquerque, New Mexico

---

## Contributing Authors

**Dr. Carol Berkin**
Professor of History
Baruch College and the
  Graduate Center
The City University of New York
New York, New York

**Lee A. Chase**
Staff Development Specialist
Chesterfield County
  Public Schools
Chesterfield County, Virginia

**Dr. Jim Cummins**
Professor of Curriculum
Ontario Institute for Studies
  in Education
University of Toronto
Toronto, Canada

**Dr. Allen D. Glenn**
Professor and Dean Emeritus
Curriculum and Instruction
College of Education
University of Washington
Seattle, Washington

**Dr. Carole L. Hahn**
Professor, Educational Studies
Emory University
Atlanta, Georgia

**Dr. M. Gail Hickey**
Professor of Education
Indiana University-Purdue
  University
Fort Wayne, Indiana

**Dr. Bonnie Meszaros**
Associate Director
Center for Economic Education
  and Entrepreneurship
University of Delaware
Newark, Delaware

ISBN 0-328-03601-3

1 2 3 4 5 6 7 8 9 10-V016-11 10 09 08 07 06 05 04 03 02

# Contents

# Lesson 1: Communities

## Vocabulary

**community** a place where people live, work, and have fun together

**geography** the study of Earth and how people live on it

## Carlos's Community

Carlos lives in the community of El Paso, Texas. A **community** is a place where people live, work, and play together. Carlos thinks his community is special for many reasons. The **geography,** or land around his community, is different from others. El Paso lies in a pass between two sets of mountains. It is also next to Mexico, the country south of the United States.

## What Is a Community?

In a community, people work together and care about one another. There are rules to follow in a community. These rules keep everyone safe. Many people have jobs in their community. They work as teachers, letter carriers, police officers, doctors, and grocery store workers or in many other jobs. All of these things are important to a community.

## History of El Paso

El Paso has a very long history. It is over 400 years old! Native Americans first lived in El Paso. Later the Spanish came. There are still many old buildings from those early days. Some special celebrations in El Paso come from Spanish history. Nearby, there is a river called the Rio Grande. Across the river is a different community that people can visit. This community is Juarez, Mexico.

## Life in El Paso

El Paso is a city. It is part of the state of Texas. Texas is part of the country of the United States of America. The United States of America is a country on the continent of North America. North America is part of the planet Earth. Families are important parts of their communities. Families of El Paso do things that families of other communities do. Some of these things are working, voting, and helping others.

# Lesson 1: Review

1. 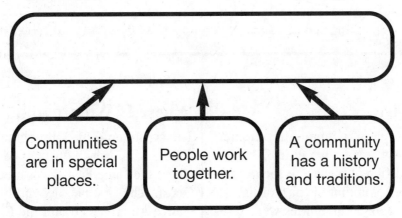 **Main Idea and Details** Fill in the main idea in the diagram below.

Communities are in special places.

People work together.

A community has a history and traditions.

2. Tell about the geography of El Paso.

_____

_____

_____

3. Tell about the history of El Paso.

_____

_____

_____

4. Name the state and country where El Paso is located.

_____

_____

_____

5. **Critical Thinking:** *Draw Conclusions* Why do you think people came to live in El Paso?

_____

_____

_____

# Lesson 2: United States Communities

## Vocabulary

| location | where something can be found |

### Where We Live

There are many types of communities. Some are small towns. Others are big cities. They are found in all different places, or **locations.** The location of a community is part of its geography. Long ago, communities were located near lakes, rivers, or oceans. People had not built good roads yet. Instead, people used boats to move people and goods. Also, farms were built on land good for growing things.

### Where Is Astoria?

Astoria, Oregon, is located where the Columbia River meets the Pacific Ocean. The community of Astoria is almost 200 years old. Many people in Astoria have parents or grandparents from a part of Europe called Scandinavia. Many people in Astoria like to boat, swim, and fish. They also like to ride waves in the Pacific Ocean. Astoria has many museums to visit.

### Where Is Wilmington?

The community of Wilmington, North Carolina, is over 250 years old. It is located where the Cape Fear River meets the Atlantic Ocean. The first people who lived there were Native Americans. Later the English came. There are interesting things to see and do in Wilmington. Airlie Gardens has birds and flowers. Many people swim in the ocean. Others explore Fort Fisher. Fort Fisher is a sand fort.

### Where Is Denver?

Denver, Colorado, is located at the foot of the Rocky Mountains. The community of Denver is near the middle of the United States. It is located where Cherry Creek meets the South Platte River. Many people like to walk in the mountains. Native Americans were the first people to live in this area. They were called the Arapaho. Later, gold was found in Denver. More people moved there to look for gold.

Name _____ Date _____

# Lesson 2: Review

1. 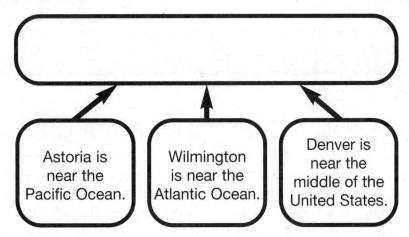 **Main Idea and Details** Fill in the main idea that tells about these communities.

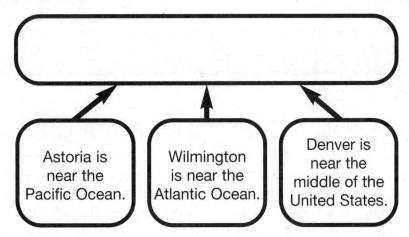

2. Why were the early communities often located near rivers or oceans?

_____

_____

_____

3. Tell about the geography of the communities of Astoria, Wilmington, and Denver.

_____

_____

_____

4. Tell about the first settlers in Astoria, Wilmington, and Denver.

_____

_____

_____

5. **Critical Thinking:** *Compare and Contrast* Compare and contrast the fun things people do in the communities of Astoria, Oregon; Wilmington, North Carolina; and Denver, Colorado.

_____

_____

_____

# Lesson 3: World Communities

## Vocabulary

**culture**  the way a group of people lives; a group's language, music, religion, food, clothing, holidays, and beliefs

## Timbuktu Long Ago

There are communities all over the world. One of these communities is Timbuktu. It is in Mali, West Africa. Between the years 1400 and 1600, Timbuktu was a very rich desert city. Thousands of people lived there. Traders brought salt and other goods to Timbuktu. They traded the salt for gold. Religion was very important in Timbuktu. In the 1500s, there was a huge university in the city. Many people went there to go to school.

## Life in Timbuktu Today

Fewer people live in Timbuktu today than long ago. Their **culture** is very different from ours in the United States. A culture is the way a group of people lives. It includes a group's language, music, religion, food, clothing, holidays, and beliefs. Many people in Mali speak the languages of Bambara and French. Their homes are made of mud bricks. There are few good roads in Mali. People travel by walking, taking buses, or riding camels. The weather in Timbuktu is hot and dry. Religion is still very important there.

# Lesson 3: Review

1. 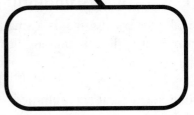 **Main Idea and Details** Fill in some details about the culture of Timbuktu.

> The culture of Timbuktu is made of many parts.

> The people speak French and Bambara.

2. Tell about what makes up the culture of a community.

_____

_____

_____

3. How is the community of Timbuktu today different from the way it was between 1400 and 1600? How is it the same?

_____

_____

_____

4. When was Timbuktu a very wealthy city?

_____

_____

_____

5. **Critical Thinking:** *Compare and Contrast* How is the community of Timbuktu today like your community? How is it different?

_____

_____

_____

# Lesson 1: A Rural Community

## Vocabulary

**rural community** a community located in the country

## Amy's Rural Community

Bridgewater, Virginia, is a small **rural community.** Rural communities are located in the country. Towns are small and far apart in the country. Open land and fields are usually found near rural communities. Bridgewater is in the state of Virginia. It is in the Shenandoah Valley. Bridgewater is in Rockingham County. It sits on the North River. About 5,000 people live in Bridgewater. A lot of its people work in larger communities that are near Bridgewater.

## Community Life

Bridgewater is small, but there is a lot to do there. People meet to talk about farming and the community. They belong to the 4-H Club. Children play sports such as baseball. They also join scouting groups. Many people like living in Bridgewater. Almost everyone in town knows and helps one another.

# Lesson 1: Review

**1.** 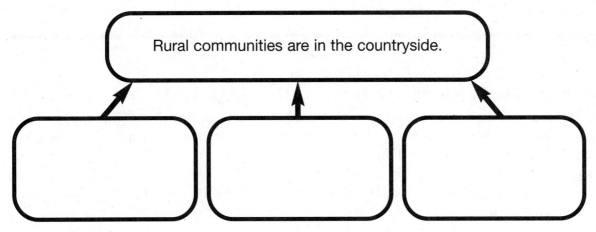 **Main Idea and Details** Fill in some of the details that tell about life in a rural community.

Rural communities are in the countryside.

**2.** What is a rural community?

_____

_____

_____

**3.** Describe the different ways that people in Bridgewater have fun.

_____

_____

_____

**4.** Describe the location of Bridgewater.

_____

_____

_____

**5.** **Critical Thinking:** *Observe* How do you think that Bridgewater might have gotten its name?

_____

_____

_____

# Lesson 2: A Suburban Community

## Vocabulary

**suburban community** a community near a large city

## Steve's Suburban Community

Levittown, New York, is a **suburban community.** Suburban communities are near large cities. Levittown is located on Long Island. Long Island is an island in the Atlantic Ocean. It is very close to New York City. New York City is the largest city in the United States. Suburban communities are also called suburbs. Many people who live in suburbs such as Levittown work in the large city nearby. People in Levittown have fun at parks and beaches.

## How Levittown Grew

Levittown was started by Abraham Levitt. He wanted to build a community where people would feel safe and comfortable. He bought a farm in 1947. Then he and his family planned and built a suburban community there. It had many homes, schools, parks, and stores. The community also had places of worship. Many people moved there from New York City. Other suburban communities were built in the United States. Highways helped suburbs grow. They let people get to work easily.

# Lesson 2: Review

1. 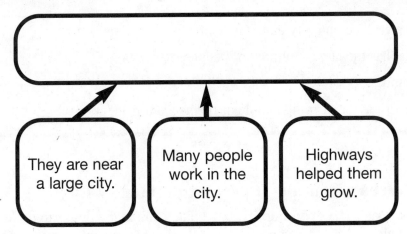 **Main Idea and Details** Fill in the main idea about suburban communities.

```
┌─────────────────────────────────────────┐
│                                         │
│                                         │
└─────────────────────────────────────────┘
```

| They are near a large city. | Many people work in the city. | Highways helped them grow. |

2. What steps did Levitt take to change a farm into a suburb?

_____

_____

_____

3. What did Levitt include in his community plan?

_____

_____

_____

4. What are some needs that lead people to form communities?

_____

_____

_____

5. **Critical Thinking:** *Observe* Tell how transportation is important to your community.

_____

_____

_____

# Lesson 3: An Urban Community

## Vocabulary

**urban community** a community that is in a city

**city** a place that has the largest number of people in an area

**population** number of people

**transportation** a way of carrying people or things from place to place

## Chicago, an Urban Community

Chicago, Illinois, is an **urban community.** An urban community is located in a **city.** Urban communities have large **populations.** The population of Chicago is more than three million people. Chicago is in the midwestern part of the United States. It is on the western shore of Lake Michigan. A fur trader moved to the area in 1779. Later, a town grew there. The town was first called Chicago in 1837.

## Working in Chicago

In Chicago, people work in many different places. They work in department stores, banks, and offices. They also work in the Sears Tower, the tallest office building in the United States. **Transportation** helps people move around the city. Transportation is important because so many people need to get to work. Many people ride on buses or the "El" train. The "El" is a raised train that runs through the city.

## Community Life

There are many things to do in Chicago. In the summer, people watch the boats on Lake Michigan. They also go to the beach or have picnics. Many people like to watch plays at the theaters in Chicago. Chicago also has many museums. Many people visit the Art Institute. The Adler Planetarium is in Chicago. Many people go there to learn about outer space. People visit the city's aquarium to learn about sea life. They also go to see the water coming out of Buckingham Fountain.

# Lesson 3: Review

1. 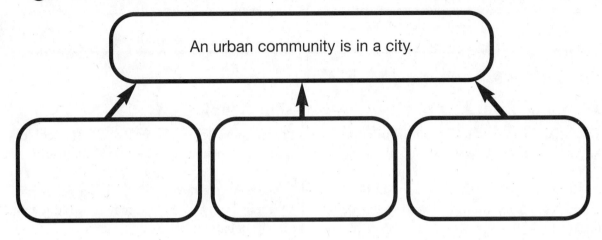 **Main Idea and Details** Fill in some details about life in an urban community.

An urban community is in a city.

2. How is an urban community different from a rural community? How is it similar?

_____

_____

_____

3. Name three fun things to do in Chicago.

_____

_____

_____

4. Name one way that people in Chicago get around that is not found in rural communities.

_____

_____

_____

5. **Critical Thinking:** *Compare and Contrast* How is a city similar to and different from its suburbs?

_____

_____

_____

Name _____ Date _____ 

Lesson 1 Summary

# Lesson 1: Moving to a New Community

Use with pages 74–77.

## Vocabulary

**opportunity** a chance for something better to happen

## We Come from All Over!

Tom's family moved to Boston from Fort Wayne, Indiana. He was worried about going to a new school. Tom felt better when he saw that some students had lived in other places. Some students came from far away to live in Boston.

## Why People Move

People move for many reasons. Some people move for a better job or a new **opportunity.** An opportunity is a chance for something better to happen. People may move to find a better life for their family. They also may move to get a better education. For many years, people have moved to the United States to be free and safe. They want to be free to help choose the government. They want to be free to follow their religion. They also want to make their children's future better. People who came to the United States made new communities here. They formed new communities to feel safer. They also wanted a better life. They set up laws to keep everyone safe. When new people move to a community, they become part of it. They must obey the laws. They can get jobs. They also make friends and go to school like everyone else. When everyone follows the laws, the community is a safe place to live.

# Lesson 1: Review

1. 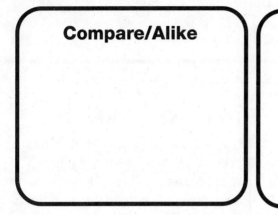 **Compare and Contrast** Fill in the diagram to compare and contrast reasons why people might move within the United States to reasons why people might move here from another country.

| Compare/Alike | Contrast/Different |
|---|---|
|  |  |

2. List reasons why people move to a new community.

_____

_____

_____

3. Why have people formed new communities?

_____

_____

_____

4. Why is it important for everyone to follow the laws of a community?

_____

_____

_____

5. **Critical Thinking:** *Draw Conclusions* What are some of the things that you can do to keep your community a good place to live?

_____

_____

_____

# Lesson 2: Learning New Customs

## Vocabulary

**immigrant** a person who moves from one country to another to live

**custom** a way of doing things

**ethnic group** a group of people with the same culture

## Moving to a New Country

Nicole's family moved to Boston, Massachusetts. They were from Haiti, a country in the Caribbean Sea. They moved to a community where other people from Haiti live. They are all **immigrants,** people who move to a new country to live. In Haiti Nicole's family spoke a language called Haitian Creole. Nicole's new friends helped her learn English. Her family still follows **customs,** or ways of doing things, from Haiti. Some things in Boston are the same as in Haiti. School is almost the same. Kids play soccer, ride buses, and also phone their friends. The neighborhood is different, though. Nicole lived in a rural community in Haiti. She lives in a city neighborhood in Boston.

## Ethnic Neighborhoods

Nicole's family is part of the Haitian **ethnic group.** An ethnic group is a group of people with the same culture. In Nicole's ethnic neighborhood, people speak in their home language. They can eat the same kind of food they ate in Haiti. They can also follow the customs of Haiti. They can learn about a new culture while still doing things from their old culture.

# Lesson 2: Review

1. 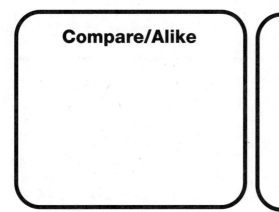 **Compare and Contrast** Fill in the diagram comparing Nicole's old community to her new one.

| Compare/Alike | Contrast/Different |
| --- | --- |
| | |

2. Why do you think Nicole's family moved to an ethnic neighborhood?

_____

_____

_____

3. Give an example of how immigrants mix some of their old culture with their new culture.

_____

_____

_____

4. What parts of their culture can immigrants find in an ethnic neighborhood?

_____

_____

_____

5. **Critical Thinking:** *Apply Information* If you moved to a new country, what do you think would be the hardest thing to learn? What would be the easiest?

_____

_____

_____

# Lesson 3: Where Did They Come From?

## Vocabulary

**ancestor** a relative who lived long ago

**symbol** an object that stands for something else

## They Came Long Ago

Nancy's **ancestors,** or relatives who lived long ago, were immigrants. They came to the United States from Europe in the early 1900s. Many other immigrants came around the same time. The first thing they saw was the Statue of Liberty in New York Bay. The statue was a **symbol** of freedom to the immigrants. A symbol is an object that stands for something else. The statue meant that their long trip was over. They could live in freedom in the United States.

## A Nation of Immigrants

Immigrants have come to the United States from almost every other country in the world. They came for freedom or opportunities. Some came because there was little food in their home country. Some came to find jobs. Some immigrants were even forced to come. Many immigrants from Europe came into the United States through New York City. Many immigrants from Asia came through San Francisco, California.

## An Immigrant Writer

Some immigrants became famous writers. These men and women told their stories through books and poems. One writer was Mary Antin. Mary came to the United States from Russia when she was twelve years old. Her family lived in Boston. She wrote a book, *The Promised Land,* about her life in Boston.

## An Immigrant Artist

Some people who came to the United States became artists. These men and women made paintings and statues. They shared their artwork with other people. Emanuel Gottlieb Leutze was born in Germany. He came to the United States when he was nine years old. He lived in Philadelphia. His most famous painting is *Washington Crossing the Delaware.* It was painted in 1851. It shows George Washington during the Revolutionary War.

# Lesson 3: Review

1. **Main Idea and Details** Fill in the main idea.

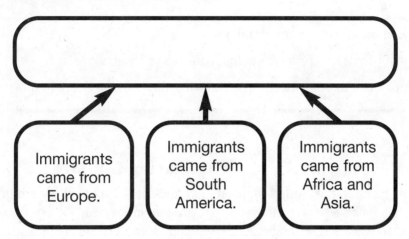

2. Why was the Statue of Liberty an important symbol to the immigrants?

_____

_____

_____

3. Where have immigrants to the United States come from?

_____

_____

_____

4. How have immigrant writers and artists shared their stories with the rest of the world?

_____

_____

_____

5. **Critical Thinking:** *Interpret Visuals* Look at the painting on page 88 in your main book. Which man is George Washington? How can you tell that he is the leader?

_____

_____

_____

# Lesson 4: A New Life in America

## Vocabulary

**citizen** an official member of a community

**migration** moving from one part of a country to live in another part

**Great Migration** when many African Americans left farms in the South to move to the North

## A New Life

Many immigrants came to the United States in the early 1900s. They had to start a new way of life. Many had to learn a new language. They also had to find homes and jobs. Some immigrants moved into ethnic neighborhoods in cities. Others worked on farms and lived in small towns. Most immigrants wanted to become citizens of the United States. A **citizen** is an official member of a country. Citizens can help make decisions for their community by voting.

## Education Past and Present

Some immigrants came from places where schools were very different. In some countries, children started school at younger ages. They learned their country's language and history. In the United States, immigrant children were taught about the way of life and government of their new country. They learned math and science. Some even learned English for the first time. Even today, schools are different in different countries. Children who come to the United States today learn things that children of the past had to learn.

## Sharing Cultures

In the early 1900s, many ethnic communities grew in cities near the oceans. As these neighborhoods grew, cities grew. Each group of immigrants brought their own customs. Later, the different customs started to mix together. The songs of one group were sung by others. People started to eat the foods of other ethnic groups. They played the games and sports of other groups.

## Moving North

Many African Americans moved from the South to the North in the early 1900s. They wanted a better way of life. This was called the **Great Migration. Migration** means moving from one part of a country to live in another part. Many African Americans left farms in the South. They moved to northern cities, such as New York City, New York; Chicago, Illinois; and Pittsburgh, Pennsylvania. They hoped to get good jobs in the factories there. When they moved, African Americans brought their culture with them. Many were musicians, writers, and artists. Some of their work became famous.

# Lesson 4: Review

1. **Main Idea and Details** Fill in the main idea.

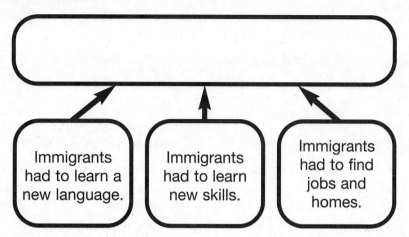

2. How can a citizen in the United States help make decisions for the community?

_____

_____

_____

3. How were schools in other countries different from those in the United States?

_____

_____

_____

4. Why did many African Americans move from the South to the North during the Great Migration?

_____

_____

_____

5. **Critical Thinking:** *Draw Conclusions* Explain how people from different cultures can help make a community special.

_____

_____

_____

# Lesson 1: Celebrating Cultures

## Vocabulary

**holiday** a special day for remembering an important person or event

**tradition** a special way a group does something

## Families Celebrate Together

Families celebrate many **holidays,** or special days, together. Some holidays are celebrated with certain **traditions.** People follow these traditions every year during a celebration. Traditions help people feel that they are part of a community. One tradition for many Asian families is to have a certain meal for Asian New Year. Some Asian communities also celebrate fall moon festivals.

## Family Celebrations

Some holidays, such as Christmas and Hanukkah, are religious. Others are not. On many holidays, families eat a meal together. Many holidays have traditions, symbols, and music. Cakes with candles are symbols that are often used to celebrate birthdays. Some families celebrate Christmas. They light candles and go to church. Many give gifts to family members. Muslim families celebrate Eid-al-Fitr. They eat a meal and special sweets. Many children get gifts. Many Jewish families celebrate Hanukkah. They light candles for eight nights. Families eat special foods. Some African American families celebrate Kwanzaa. They light seven candles. Each candle stands for something special.

## Communities Celebrate Cultures

Many communities celebrate holidays from other cultures. For example, Cinco de Mayo is a Mexican holiday. It celebrates a special day. On this day the Mexicans won a battle against the French. Many people around the world celebrate Cinco de Mayo. They wear colorful clothes. They play music and eat Mexican food. St. Patrick's Day is another holiday. It is celebrated in many places. It began as a religious holiday in Ireland. This is a day to celebrate Irish culture. Some people wear green clothes. They may go to a parade or eat green food.

Name ______________________ Date ____________

**Lesson 1 Review**

Use with pages 104–109.

# Lesson 1: Review

1. **Compare and Contrast** Fill in the diagram with more facts to compare and contrast family celebrations and community celebrations.

| Compare/Alike | Contrast/Different |
| --- | --- |
| | |

2. Why do people celebrate holidays?

______________________________________________

______________________________________________

______________________________________________

3. Why do groups of people follow traditions?

______________________________________________

______________________________________________

______________________________________________

4. Tell how people in other countries and in the United States celebrate ethnic holidays such as Cinco de Mayo and St. Patrick's Day.

______________________________________________

______________________________________________

______________________________________________

5. **Critical Thinking:** ***Apply Information*** Tell how you celebrate events that are important to you.

______________________________________________

______________________________________________

______________________________________________

# Lesson 2: Celebrating a Community's Past

## Vocabulary

**livestock** farm animals raised on local farms

## Community Celebrations

Many communities have celebrations for important people or events. These celebrations help bring the community together. One example of a community celebration is a fair. Communities hold community fairs or state fairs. These fairs bring community members together. Some communities hold heritage festivals. These festivals honor the history and culture of the people who live there. New Orleans, Louisiana, has a famous heritage festival. Some communities celebrate Founder's Day. This day honors the people who started the community.

## Kansas State Fair

State fairs celebrate the work people have done all year. People from all over Kansas show their best work at the state fair. The state fair is held in September. That is when the crops are ready to eat. Farmers bring **livestock,** or farm animals, to show. Other people show homemade arts and crafts. Some show plants, vegetables, and baked goods. People judge many of these things. The winners get ribbons.

## Remembering Their Past

Some communities celebrate events from long ago. San Antonio, Texas, celebrates the Battle of the Alamo. During this battle, Texas settlers fought the Mexican Army.

# Lesson 2: Review

1.  **Compare and Contrast** Fill in the diagram with facts to compare and contrast kinds of community celebrations.

| Compare/Alike | Contrast/Different |
|---|---|
|  |  |

2. Why do some communities have a heritage festival?

_____

_____

_____

3. When do state fairs usually take place?

_____

_____

_____

4. What is one reason why state fairs take place?

_____

_____

_____

5. **Critical Thinking:** *Apply Information* Why do communities celebrate their history?

_____

_____

_____

# Lesson 3: Celebrations Across Our Nation

## Vocabulary

**Civil Rights Movement** a drive for all people to be treated the same

## Holidays for Freedom

Many holidays honor freedom in the United States. Memorial Day honors people who fought and died in wars for freedom. Veterans Day honors people who fought for freedom. Martin Luther King Day also celebrates a fight for freedom. Dr. King led the **Civil Rights Movement.** This was a drive for all people to be treated the same. Dr. King used words to fight. He did not believe in violence. He wanted fair treatment of African Americans.

## Being Thankful

Thanksgiving Day is another American holiday. People give thanks for the good things that happened that year. The settlers of Plymouth, Massachusetts, celebrated one of the first Thanksgivings in 1621. These settlers were called Pilgrims. Pilgrims had come from England to be free to practice their own religion. Their first winter had been very hard. The next fall, the Pilgrims wanted to give thanks to God. They were thankful for their good crops and for living through the winter. They also wanted to thank a group of Wampanoag Indians who had helped them. Today, we give thanks for what we have. Families celebrate by having a special meal together.

# Lesson 3: Review

1. **Main Idea and Details** Fill in the diagram to show more details about the main idea.

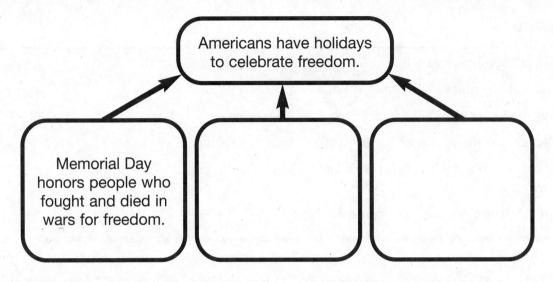

Americans have holidays
to celebrate freedom.

Memorial Day
honors people who
fought and died in
wars for freedom.

2. What was the Civil Rights Movement?

_____

_____

_____

3. How did Dr. Martin Luther King, Jr., try to make changes in the United States?

_____

_____

_____

4. Why did the Pilgrims come to America?

_____

_____

_____

5. **Critical Thinking:** *Make Inferences* Why did the Pilgrims need help from the Wampanoag?

_____

_____

_____

# Lesson 1: What Is Your Community's Environment?

## Vocabulary

**region** a large land area that is different from the areas around it

**physical environment** the landforms and climate of a place

**climate** the kind of weather a place has from year to year

**landform** a shape or part of Earth's surface, such as a mountain or plain

**ecosystem** a community of plants and animals working together with their physical environment

**adapt** to change the way you do something

## Katrinka's Western Community

Katrinka lives in Bozeman, Montana. Katrinka walks in the nearby mountains. She likes to fish in the nearby rivers. Montana is in the Western **region** of the United States. A region is a large land area. Each region is special. Regions have different **landforms.** Landforms are parts of Earth's surface. Mountains and plains are landforms. Regions also have different **climates.** Climate is the kind of weather a place has from year to year. A region's landforms and climate are part of its **physical environment.**

## Communities in the Regions

People live in communities in all regions of the United States. The land around each community looks different. Different plants and animals live in each region. The land, plants, and animals form an **ecosystem.** In an ecosystem, plants and animals work together with their physical environment. A river is a kind of ecosystem. So are a forest and a desert. People use the physical environments of their communities. Stamford, Connecticut, is in the Northeast region. People walk in the nearby hills and forests. They may see deer and snakes. Charleston, South Carolina, is in the Southeast region. People there ride boats on rivers. They may see rice fields and birds. There also are many trees. Omaha, Nebraska, is in the Midwest region. There also are rivers in this area. People ride bikes on the flat land. They sometimes hear coyotes. Tucson, Arizona, is in the Southwest region. People there see canyons, deserts, rivers, and mountains. They can walk in parks. They may see cactuses, snakes, and desert toads.

## Changes in People and Places

People **adapt** to their physical environment. Adapt means to change the way you do something. Adapting helps people live in certain places. In cold places, people heat buildings and wear warm clothes. People also change the environment to meet their needs. They cut down trees and forests to build houses. They build roads to move people and goods. People build cities and railroads. They bring water to very dry places to grow crops.

Name _____     Date _____

# Lesson 1: Review

1. **⟳ Draw Conclusions** Choose a community from this lesson. Use the details you read about to draw a conclusion about how the physical environment affects life in the community.

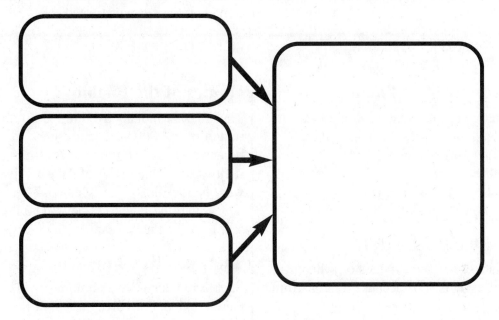

2. What makes up the physical environment of a region?

   _____

   _____

3. List five regions of the United States and tell about their physical environments.

   _____

   _____

4. How do people adapt to and change their environment?

   _____

   _____

5. **Critical Thinking:** *Predict* How might building a large new highway affect a rural community?

   _____

   _____

# Lesson 2: Living in Different Climates

## Vocabulary

**adobe** a mixture of earth, straw, and water that is made into bricks and dried

## What Makes Up Climate?

The United States has many different climates. Climate is the weather a place has year after year. Temperature is a part of climate. Temperature is how hot or cold something is. How much rain or snow falls is part of climate too. So is how strongly the winds blow.

## United States Climates

The climate of a place depends on where it is. Barrow, Alaska, is cold because it is far from the equator. Places that are far from the equator are cold. Places that are near the equator are warm. Kauai, Hawaii, is near the equator. It is warm all year. The climate of a place also depends on how high it is. Very high places can be cold. Mountains can have snow all year. Being near very large lakes or oceans may also affect climates. People adapt to their climate. They wear clothes to keep them cool or warm. They build homes that keep them safe.

## Homes of the Pueblo

The Anasazi Indians lived in the Southwest region over 2,000 years ago. Some of their homes were built into cliffs. A cliff is a steep, rocky slope. One group of Anasazi lived in what is now Taos, New Mexico. This group is now called the Pueblo Indians. The Pueblo still live like the Anasazi in many ways.

## Taos and Its Climate

Pueblo Indians have a community in Taos, New Mexico. They live on a high flat area with mountains around it. The climate is dry. In summer, Taos has warm days and cool nights. In winter, the weather can be cold. Snow falls often. The Pueblo adapted to this climate. They built houses from **adobe.** Adobe is a mixture of earth, straw, and water. It is made into bricks and dried. Adobe houses keep people warm in winter and cool in summer.

# Lesson 2: Review

1. 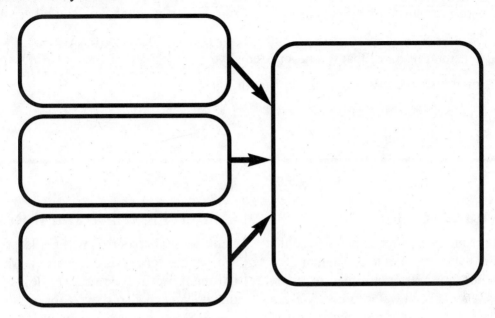 **Draw Conclusions** Use details to draw a conclusion about how you adapt to the climate where you live.

2. What are the different parts of the climate of a place?

_____

_____

3. What causes the climate of some places to be warm and other places to be cold?

_____

_____

4. How have people in the Pueblo Indian community in Taos, New Mexico, adapted to the climate?

_____

_____

5. **Critical Thinking:** *Evaluate* In which type of climate would you rather live? Why?

_____

_____

# Lesson 3: Communities and Resources

## Vocabulary

**natural resources** useful materials that come from the earth; water, soil, and oil are natural resources

**mineral** a natural resource that has never been alive

**fuel** a natural resource that is burned for heat or light

**conserve** to use something carefully

**recycle** to use something again

## Our Natural Resources

**Natural resources** are things people use that come from the earth. People use natural resources for food. Water and soil are natural resources. People need water to live. We grow food in soil. Natural resources such as trees are used to build homes. **Minerals** are natural resources that were never alive. Gold and salt are minerals. **Fuels** are natural resources too. A fuel is something that is burned for heat or light. Oil and gas are fuels.

## Mineral Resources

In 1848 gold was found in California. Thousands of people rushed there. They wanted to find gold. This movement was called the Gold Rush. People looked for gold in muddy streams. They dug deep into the earth. Many people stayed in communities in California after the Gold Rush ended. Oil is another important natural resource. In 1901 oil was found in Beaumont, Texas. Many people moved to this Texas community. They wanted to work in the oil fields. Oil is still important in Texas today. Alaska is another state where oil is important. People use oil to make motor oil and gasoline for cars. People also use oil to make plastics.

## Conserving Our Natural Resources

Some natural resources will not last forever. We can **conserve** these resources. We should use them carefully. We can use less of some things. We can also **recycle,** or use things again. Some things can be recycled and made into new products. Paper is one of these things. We can take better care of some resources, such as soil. Fuels are natural resources that can be used up. We can conserve fuels by using them carefully.

# Lesson 3: Review

**1.** ⟳ **Draw Conclusions** Use the details you read about to draw a conclusion about the importance of conserving natural resources.

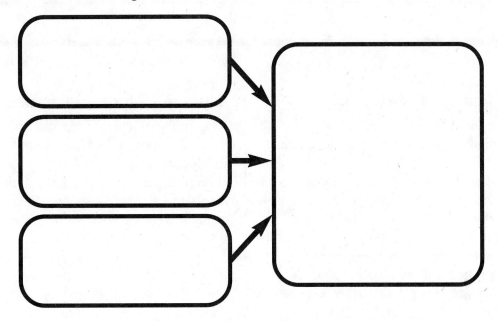

**2.** Describe some important natural resources.

_____

_____

**3.** How has the discovery of natural resources changed communities?

_____

_____

**4.** What are some ways that people can conserve resources?

_____

_____

**5. Critical Thinking:** *Observe* Why do you think the use of oil has increased since 1901?

_____

_____

# Lesson 1: A Mountain Community

## Vocabulary

**miner** a person who digs materials from the earth

## How Glenwood Springs Grew

Long ago, the Ute Indians lived in Colorado. They settled on land in the mountains. Today, the town of Glenwood Springs is located here. The Ute Indians found hot water springs in Glenwood Canyon. The springs made their aches and pains feel better. In 1879 other people came to live there. **Miners** came to dig up coal from the earth. Some people came for the hot springs. In 1881 Captain Isaac Cooper set up Fort Defiance. The town's name was changed to Glenwood Springs. In 1887 the railroad came through the Rocky Mountains to Glenwood Springs. This gave miners a way to send out coal. People also rode the train to visit the hot springs.

## Living in Mountain Communities

Living in the mountains was difficult. It was hard to travel in the mountains. It was hard to grow food on the land in mountains. However, the early communities in the Rocky Mountains had many resources. People started mountain communities in other parts of the United States too.

# Lesson 1: Review

1. ⟳ **Draw Conclusions** Use the details you read about Glenwood Springs. Draw a conclusion about why people settled there.

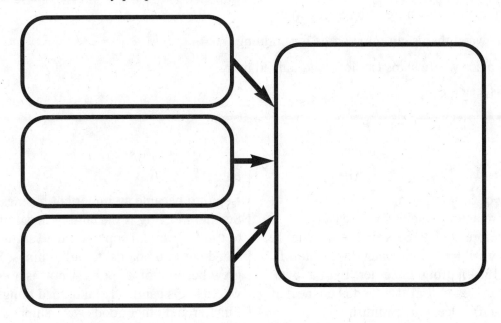

2. What events changed Glenwood Springs over time?

_____

_____

3. What natural resource brings visitors to Glenwood Springs?

_____

_____

4. What made it difficult to live in mountain communities?

_____

_____

5. **Critical Thinking:** *Compare and Contrast* Why did the Utes and the settlers come to the Glenwood Springs area? How were their reasons similar and different?

_____

_____

# Lesson 2: A Water Community

## Vocabulary

**logging** cutting down trees to use for wood

**lumber** wood that is cut into boards for building

**port** a place where ships can load and unload things

**industries** kinds of businesses

## The Early Days of Seattle

The city of Seattle has many rolling hills. There also are mountains to the east and south. Before the city of Seattle grew, the area had many tall trees. The waters were full of fish. In 1851 a group of settlers built a town near Puget Sound. Puget Sound is connected to the Pacific Ocean. Duwamish and Suquamish Indians lived in the area. One of the Native American leaders was Chief Seathl. He was friendly to settlers and helped them. The settlers named their town Seattle after Chief Seathl. People told tall tales about how Puget Sound was formed. One of these stories is about a giant man named Paul Bunyan. The story says that Bunyan dug out land to make Puget Sound.

## Seattle Today

**Logging** became an important business in Seattle. Logging is the cutting down of trees to use for wood. People use the **lumber,** or wood cut into boards, to build things. Seattle grew because of its **port.** A port is a place where ships can load and unload things. Lumber and other goods were shipped to and from Seattle. New **industries** have come to Seattle. Industries are kinds of businesses. Today, Seattle is known for airplane making and computer companies. Some people now worry about what will happen to Seattle's natural resources.

# Lesson 2: Review

1. 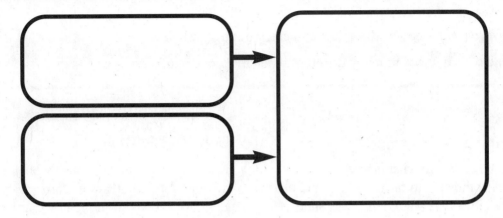 **Draw Conclusions** Use the details you read about Seattle. Draw a conclusion about the good and bad effects of Seattle's growth.

2. Describe a person and an event that changed Seattle.

_____

_____

_____

3. Describe the physical environment and the natural resources around Seattle.

_____

_____

_____

4. In what way were wood and water important natural resources in the growth of Seattle?

_____

_____

_____

5. **Critical Thinking:** *Predict* How do you think Seattle will change if its population continues to grow quickly?

_____

_____

_____

# Lesson 3: A Crossroads Community

## Vocabulary

**state capital**   a city where a state government is located

**state government**  people who make and carry out a state's laws

**crossroads**  a place where many different roads meet one another

## Forming the Crossroads

White settlers came to what is now Indianapolis, Indiana, to farm. In 1820 people picked the city as the **state capital.** A state capital is a city where the **state government** is located. People in state government make and carry out a state's laws. In the 1830s the first highway in the United States came through Indianapolis. The highway was called the National Road. It helped people move from east to west. More roads were built. Indianapolis became known as the "Crossroads of America." A **crossroads** is a place where many different roads meet.

## Roads and Railroads

You cannot get to Indianapolis by boat. But many important highways go through the city. Trucks carry goods from the city to other parts of the country. The railroad came to Indianapolis in 1847. It brought many people to Indianapolis. The Union Rail Station was built in 1852. Indianapolis became an important stop for many railroad lines. The **Underground Railroad** also stopped in Indianapolis. It was not a real railroad. It was a way for African American slaves to get to freedom in the North. The Underground Railroad was made up of a group of places for people to stop. One stop was Bethel AME Church in Indianapolis. Some people in the church helped the slaves escape.

# Lesson 3: Review

1. **Draw Conclusions** Use details from the lesson. Draw a conclusion about the importance of Indianapolis in the past and present.

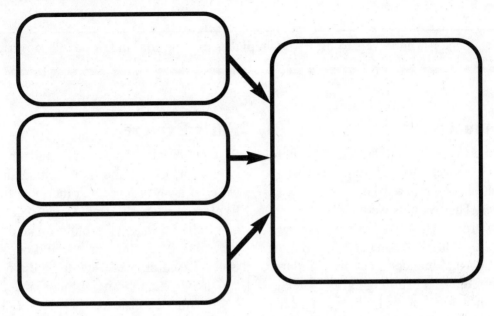

2. Why is Indianapolis known as the "Crossroads of America"?

_____

_____

3. What events were important to Indianapolis's early growth?

_____

_____

4. What made Indianapolis an important stop on the Underground Railroad?

_____

_____

5. **Critical Thinking:** *Evaluate* Why do you think so many roads were built through Indianapolis?

_____

_____

# Lesson 1: Explorers Come to North America

## Vocabulary

**explorer** a person who travels to little-known places looking for land or new discoveries

## The Iroquois

Native Americans lived in the Americas before European **explorers** arrived. Explorers are people who look for new lands or other discoveries. The Iroquois were a Native American group. They lived in what is now New York and Quebec, Canada. The Iroquois were farmers and hunters. They lived in large, wooden buildings called longhouses. They cut wood for their longhouses in the spring. That was when the wood was green and easy to bend. The Iroquois had a government. They had rules that protected the rights of their people. The rules also protected their ways of worship. In time, explorers from Spain, England, and France came to the Americas. The Europeans had different beliefs and ideas from the Native Americans. The differences sometimes led to problems.

## Early Explorers

Portugal, Spain, France, and England traded goods with China and India. China and India were far away from these other countries. Explorers wanted to find a way to get to China and India by water. Traveling by land took a long time. They thought it would be faster by water. Explorers were sent to find a route to China and India. Some of them landed in North America instead. They explored North America. Some built settlements. Some people who explored North America for Spain were Christopher Columbus, Hernando de Soto, and Juan Ponce de León. French explorers were Jacques Cartier and Samuel de Champlain. England sent John Cabot and Henry Hudson.

# Lesson 1: Review

1. Cause and Effect Fill in the effects for each of the causes.

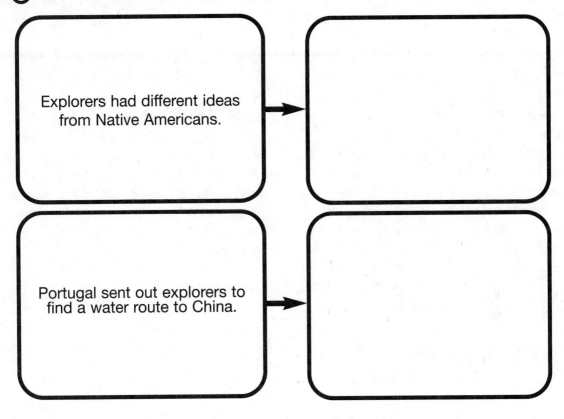

Explorers had different ideas from Native Americans. ➔

Portugal sent out explorers to find a water route to China. ➔

2. Why did the Iroquois cut wood for their houses in the spring?

_____

_____

3. What rights did the Iroquois form of government protect?

_____

_____

4. Name four countries that sent explorers to the Americas.

_____

_____

5. **Critical Thinking: _Draw Conclusions_** Why do you think that the countries that traded with China and India wanted a water route to those countries?

_____

_____

# Lesson 2: A Spanish Community

## Vocabulary

**fleet** a large group of ships

## The Spanish in Florida

Juan Ponce de León was a Spanish explorer. He landed in what is now Florida. He called it *La Florida*. This means "land of flowers." Ponce de León was searching for riches. Instead he found great farmland. Ponce de León was disappointed and went back to Spain. He came back to Florida in 1521. He brought a group of settlers. He hoped to build a city. Fighting broke out between the Spanish and the native people. Ponce de León was killed.

## The Fight for Florida

The French also wanted to settle Florida. They set up a fort near where the Spanish had first landed. The king of Spain sent Don Pedro Menéndez de Avilés to explore and settle Florida. Menéndez and his settlers built a fort and settlement. They named it St. Augustine. The French and Spanish fought to control the coast of Florida. The Spanish took the French fort. They also defeated the French **fleet,** or group of ships. St. Augustine became the first permanent European settlement in North America.

## St. Augustine Today

St. Augustine, Florida, is one of the oldest communities in the United States. It has many beaches. It has the oldest standing house in the United States. It also has the oldest stone fort in the country. The people of St. Augustine have kept the Spanish culture of the community alive.

# Lesson 2: Review

1. ⟳ **Cause and Effect** For each cause, fill in the effect in the correct box.

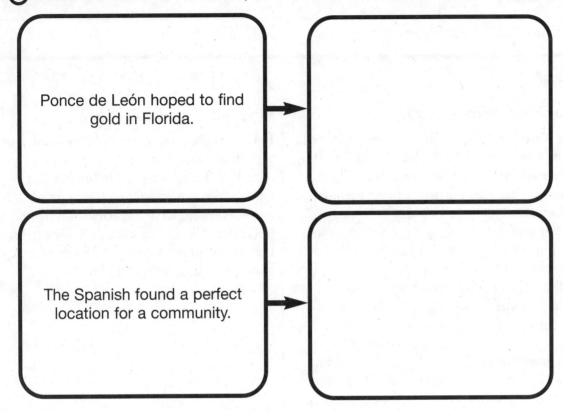

Ponce de León hoped to find gold in Florida. →

The Spanish found a perfect location for a community. →

2. What does *La Florida* mean in English?

_____

_____

3. Why did Ponce de León come back to Florida in 1521?

_____

_____

4. What two countries fought over Florida in the 1500s?

_____

_____

5. **Critical Thinking: *Draw Conclusions*** How can you tell that people who live in St. Augustine today are proud of their history?

_____

_____

# Lesson 3: A French Community

## Vocabulary

**fortification** a wall that protects an object or a building

## The French in Canada

The French wanted to find a faster trade route to the East. They thought they could find it by traveling north and west on rivers and lakes. They sent Jacques Cartier to find the route. In 1534 he landed on present-day Newfoundland. Cartier realized that he had not found a route to China. Waterfalls and rapids blocked the path west. Cartier went back to France. In 1608 Samuel de Champlain sailed from France to what is now Canada. He built a permanent French settlement called Quebec City. Quebec City was a good place for a settlement. It was on a hill. The St. Lawrence River was good for travel and trade. During the next 150 years, many battles were fought for Quebec City. In 1759 the English took over. French rule in Canada ended.

## Quebec City Today

In Old Quebec, there are old stone walls, or **fortifications.** That is where the French built their fort. There is a park in the old part of Quebec. People go to the park to watch musicians, jugglers, and artists. Many people in Quebec City speak French. They celebrate French customs and traditions. Quebec City's culture makes it a special place.

# Lesson 3: Review

1. 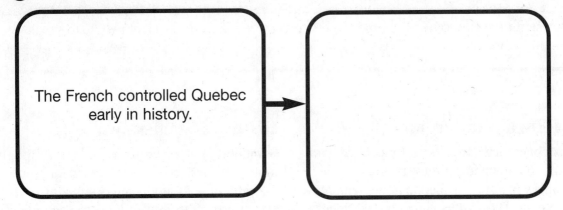 **Cause and Effect** Look at the cause. Fill in the effect in the box.

The French controlled Quebec early in history. →

2. Why did Champlain build a permanent settlement at Quebec City?

_____

_____

3. Where did Cartier first land when he arrived in the Americas?

_____

_____

4. What culture makes Quebec City special?

_____

_____

5. **Critical Thinking:** *Make Inferences* Why would rapids and waterfalls cause Cartier to turn back from his search for a route to China and India?

_____

_____

# Lesson 4: An English Community

## Vocabulary

**representative government** a type of government in which voters elect people to speak for them

## The English in Virginia

Christopher Newport was an English captain. In 1607 he dropped off the first settlers from his ship. They named their settlement Jamestown. The settlers came to find riches. But they faced problems. They quickly ran out of food. John Smith was a leader in the settlement. He went to look for food. Native Americans had lived in this place for a long time. The Native American chief, Powhatan, agreed to help the settlers. Smith went back to the settlement. But only about 38 people out of 105 were still alive. The others had died of hunger or disease.

## History of Jamestown

Soon 400 more settlers arrived. They brought more supplies. Then a fire destroyed much of the settlement. Later, John Smith was hurt. He went back to England. From September 1609 to May 1610, the settlement faced "the starving time." Many people died because they had no food. But then another ship landed and saved the town. The men in Jamestown had the same rights they had in England. One of these rights let them have a say in how they were governed. In 1619 settlers held the first representative assembly, a type of meeting. They met to form a **representative government.** In a representative government, voters elect leaders. The leaders speak for the people. The Jamestown government worked for all the people of Virginia.

## Jamestown Today

Jamestown is a national historic site. People from all over the world come to visit. They want to learn the history of this important settlement.

Name _____  Date _____

# Lesson 4: Review

1. **Cause and Effect** For each cause, fill in the effect in the correct box.

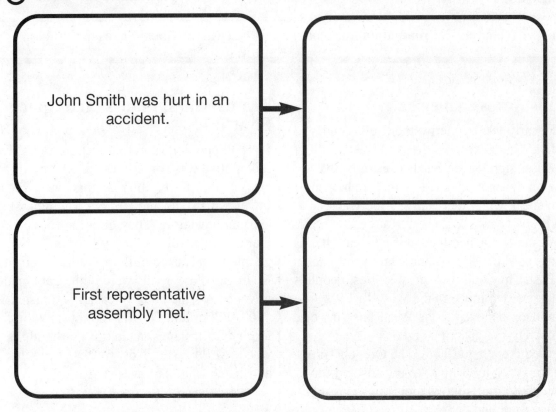

John Smith was hurt in an accident. →

First representative assembly met. →

2. How did Christopher Newport help found Jamestown?

_____

_____

3. What was "the starving time"?

_____

_____

4. What was one right that some of the men brought with them to Jamestown?

_____

_____

5. **Critical Thinking:** *Make Inferences* Do you think that the settlers who came to Jamestown were prepared? Why or why not?

_____

_____

# Lesson 1: Transportation Over Time

## Vocabulary

**Transcontinental Railroad** train lines that linked the eastern United States to the West

## Trails Across America

In the early 1800s, Meriwether Lewis and William Clark explored the land west of the Mississippi River. Sacagawea, a Native American woman, helped them. She helped them speak with other Native Americans. Lewis and Clark crossed the Rocky Mountains. They finally reached the Pacific Ocean. It was a long, hard trip. Lewis and Clark went back to the East. They told wonderful stories. People then wanted to move to the West. In 1842 many people moved to the West. They traveled in covered wagons pulled by oxen. They followed the Oregon Trail. The Oregon Trail was first used by Native Americans and fur traders. The trip took six months. It was full of hard work and danger.

## Westward Expansion

More people headed west. They wanted to find riches. Families joined together in wagon trains. But people needed a better, safer way to travel. The steam locomotive changed the way people traveled. Soon railroad companies began to lay tracks across the country. In 1869 the **Transcontinental Railroad** was finished. This railway linked the eastern United States to the West.

## Trains, Cars, Planes, and Space Shuttles

In 1830 people began to travel on trains. The locomotive was sometimes called the "Iron Horse." It replaced the real horse as a way to travel. Karl Benz and Gottlieb Daimler were German inventors. They built the first cars that ran on gasoline. Henry Ford and other people then started building cars in Detroit, Michigan. New roads were built. Cars made travel across the country easier and faster. In 1903 Wilbur and Orville Wright flew the first airplane. Airplanes made travel around the whole world faster. Now rockets, satellites, and space shuttles travel in space.

# Lesson 1: Review

1. 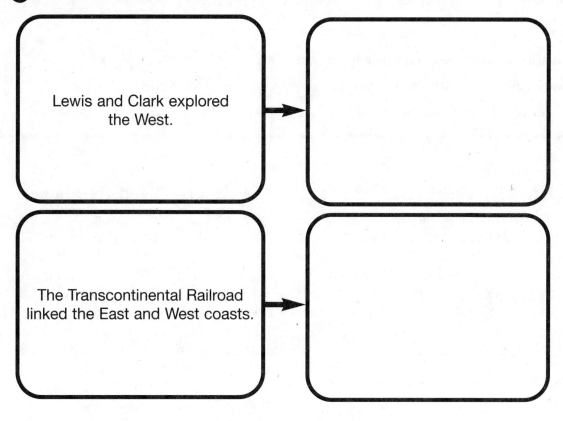 **Cause and Effect** For each cause, fill in the effect in the correct box.

Lewis and Clark explored
the West.

→

The Transcontinental Railroad
linked the East and West coasts.

→

2. Which group of people first traveled along the Oregon Trail?

_____

_____

3. How did families traveling to the West on the Oregon Trail move their belongings?

_____

_____

4. What new form of transportation was the result of an invention by Orville and Wilbur Wright?

_____

_____

5. **Critical Thinking:** *Make Inferences* Why do you think the Iron Horse replaced the real horse as a way to travel to the West?

_____

_____

# Lesson 2: Communication Over Time

## Vocabulary

**Pony Express** a mail service in which riders carried mail on horseback

**invention** something that is made for the first time

**Morse code** a way of signaling in which dots and dashes stand for letters

**broadcast** to send out information

## Mail by Horseback

In 1775 Benjamin Franklin was in charge of the postal service, or mail. Mail sent within a city arrived pretty quickly. If mail was sent far away, it could take weeks. In the 1800s mail was sent by horseback or wagon train. Many people had moved to the West. It was hard for them to communicate with friends and family in the East.

## Mail by Pony Express

In the 1800s people did not always get their mail. Sometimes robbers attacked mail wagons. Weather also caused problems. In 1860 a group of people found a way to deliver mail faster and more safely. They set up the **Pony Express.** It delivered mail to the West. Mail carriers rode horses 75 miles per day. The Pony Express cut mail delivery time in half. Then the Transcontinental Railroad was built. The postal service then sent mail across country on the train. The Transcontinental Railroad put an end to the Pony Express.

## The Telegraph and Telephone

In 1837 Samuel Morse invented a machine that could send and receive messages. The machine sent signals through a thin wire. Morse called his **invention** the telegraph. An invention is something that is made for the first time. In 1861 a telegraph wire connected the eastern and western parts of the United States. People used the telegraph to send messages across the country in seconds. The signals on the telegraph were in **Morse code.** In Morse code, dots and dashes stand for letters. In 1876 Alexander Graham Bell invented the telephone. Like the telegraph, the telephone used wires. Now, people in different places could talk to each other easily.

## Radio and Television

In 1896 Guglielmo Marconi found a way for voices to travel over long distances with no wires. His invention was the radio. People got information from the radio. In 1908 A. A. Campbell Swinton built a television. Words and pictures could be **broadcast,** or sent out. At first, the pictures were black and white. Now they are in color. Communication has changed even more in the past 20 years. Some telephones no longer need wires. Satellites and cables send hundreds of television channels. The Internet lets messages arrive in seconds.

# Lesson 2: Review

1. 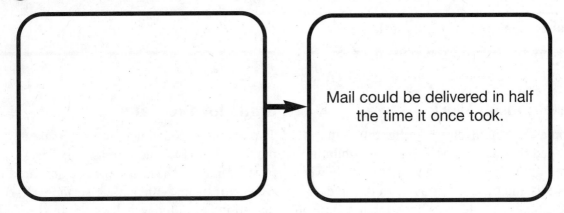 **Cause and Effect** Look at the effect. Fill in the cause in the box.

Mail could be delivered in half the time it once took.

2. Why was the Pony Express set up in 1860?

_____

_____

_____

3. How did Samuel Morse and Alexander Graham Bell change the way people communicated?

_____

_____

_____

4. Why was radio such an important invention?

_____

_____

_____

5. **Critical Thinking:** *Draw Conclusions* Why is it important to be able to communicate easily?

_____

_____

_____

# Lesson 3: Inventions Over Time

## Vocabulary

**reaper** a machine that cuts grain

## Inventions at Work

Thomas Edison invented the lightbulb. It changed the way people lived. The lightbulb gave light with little danger of fire. It allowed factories and offices to stay open day and night. Louis Latimer was an African American inventor. He worked with Thomas Edison and Alexander Graham Bell. Latimer invented many of the parts in lightbulbs and lamps that we use today. His work helped bring electric light to New York City, Philadelphia, and other cities.

## Inventions in Farming

In the 1700s and 1800s, many people worked on farms. The work was hard. Harvesting was difficult. A person would walk though the field carrying a sharp blade with a long handle. The person would swing the blade to cut the grain. In 1831 Cyrus Hall McCormick invented the **reaper,** a machine that cuts grain. The reaper made harvesting crops easier.

## Smile for the Camera

Two inventors found new ways to make pictures. Louis Daguerre made his first photographs in 1831. The picture appeared on a piece of metal with a silver surface. His invention led to today's photography. In 1888 George Eastman made a simple camera. He put everything a person needed to take a picture into a box.

## The Information Age

In the last 20 years, inventors have changed the way people work and play. Compact discs, DVD players, CD players, cell phones, and tiny pocket computers are used every day.

# Lesson 3: Review

1. 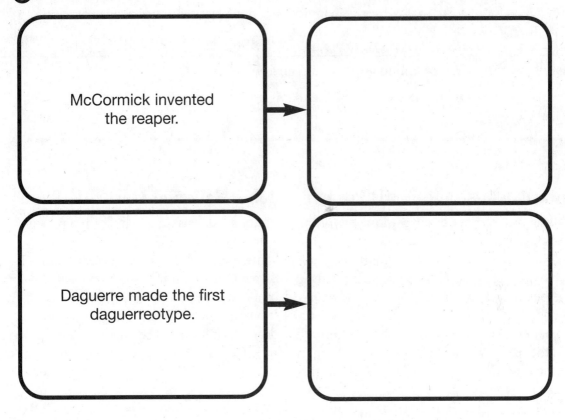 **Cause and Effect** For each cause, fill in the effect in the correct box.

McCormick invented the reaper.

→

Daguerre made the first daguerreotype.

→

2. How did Lewis Latimer help New York City and Philadelphia?

_____

_____

3. How did farmers harvest crops before McCormick invented the reaper?

_____

_____

4. What current inventions were made possible by the inventions of Daguerre and Eastman?

_____

_____

5. **Critical Thinking:** *Evaluate* What computer inventions do you use every day? Which do you think is the most important? Why?

_____

_____

# Lesson 4: Medicine Improves Over Time

## Vocabulary

**pasteurization** a way of killing germs using heat

**vaccine** a weak or killed form of a disease that is given to people so that they do not get the disease

## Edward Jenner and Louis Pasteur

Smallpox is a terrible disease. Many people used to die from it. Edward Jenner of England worked to protect people from smallpox. He noticed something in 1796. He noticed that some people never got smallpox. Those people had once had a disease called cowpox. Jenner gave patients some very weak cowpox germs. Then the patients' bodies learned to fight off smallpox. Louis Pasteur of France learned that germs cause many diseases. If disease germs could not enter a person's body, the person would not get the disease. Pasteur came up with a way to kill certain germs in milk. He heated the milk. We call this process **pasteurization.** This made milk safe to drink.

## Jonas Salk and Gertrude Elion

Polio is a disease that can harm a person's spinal cord. In 1952 Jonas Salk made something to protect people from polio. It was a **vaccine.** A vaccine is a weak or killed form of a disease that is given to people. Salk used Edward Jenner's ideas. He gave patients some dead polio germs. The vaccine stopped people from getting polio. Doctors also try to make sick people well. In the 1940s Gertrude Elion found a way to treat some diseases. Her medicines attacked certain diseased cells. They did not harm healthy cells. These medicines saved many lives. Elion won the Nobel Prize for her work. Today medicines save many lives. Many diseases are nearly gone. People are living longer, healthier lives.

# Lesson 4: Review

1. ⟳ **Cause and Effect** For each cause, fill in the effect in the correct box.

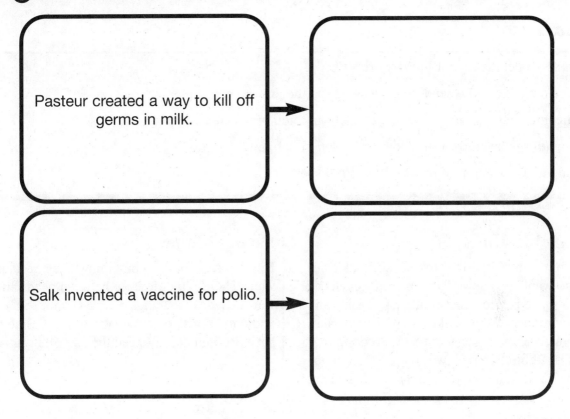

Pasteur created a way to kill off germs in milk.

Salk invented a vaccine for polio.

2. Describe the most important step in the process of pasteurization.

_____

_____

3. How is polio prevented?

_____

_____

4. What prize did Gertrude Elion earn for her work?

_____

_____

5. **Critical Thinking:** *Draw Conclusions* How did Edward Jenner figure out how to prevent smallpox?

_____

_____

# Lesson 1: Earning, Spending, and Saving

## Vocabulary

**earn** to get money for doing work

**budget** a plan for spending and saving the money you earn

**income** all the money a person earns from a job or in other ways

**spending** the amount of income a person uses to buy things

**saving** the amount of income that is not spent

## Earning Money

Robin wants a new bat to play softball. She also wants two new CDs. She must **earn** the money to pay for the bat and CDs. She can earn money if she works and gets paid. She knows the bat costs about $35. So do the two CDs. Robin thinks of ways to earn the money. She could walk the neighbor's dog. She could also weed her parents' garden.

## Keeping Track of Money

Next, Robin makes a **budget** to help her buy the bat. A budget is a plan that shows **income, spending,** and **saving.** Robin's income is the money she makes from her jobs and allowance. Her income is $6 a week. Robin buys a snack for $1 once a week. Her spending is $1 a week. The money that she has left over is her savings. Her savings is $5 a week. Robin must save for seven weeks to get $35.

## Saving Money

People save money to buy things they need and want. There is a difference between needs and wants. Needs are things people cannot live without. Wants are things people would like to have. Robin does not need the bat. She wants it.

# Lesson 1: Review

1. 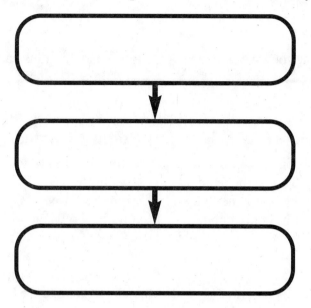 **Sequence** Sequence some of the steps Robin used to save money.

2. What are some things Robin can do each week to earn money?

_____

_____

3. How is saving different from income?

_____

_____

4. What are some examples of needs and wants?

_____

_____

5. **Critical Thinking:** *Draw Conclusions* What are some ways that Robin could save more money?

_____

_____

# Lesson 2: Choosing Wisely

## Vocabulary

**economic choice** something a person chooses to buy

**opportunity cost** what you give up when you choose one thing instead of another

## People Make Choices

People make a choice when they pick one thing instead of another. People make an **economic choice** when they buy one thing instead of another. Robin has only enough money to buy either a bat or two CDs. Robin must make a choice.

## Robin's Choice

Robin chose to buy a bat. She decided not to buy the two CDs. The two CDs were Robin's **opportunity cost.** Opportunity cost is what you give up when you choose one thing instead of another. Then Robin had to decide which bat to buy. She used a chart to show her possible choices. She thought about how much each bat weighed. She also thought about how long each bat will last. The chart helped show Robin what was important to her. Then she chose a bat to buy.

# Lesson 2: Review

1. **Main Idea and Details** List the choices Robin must make as she chooses a bat.

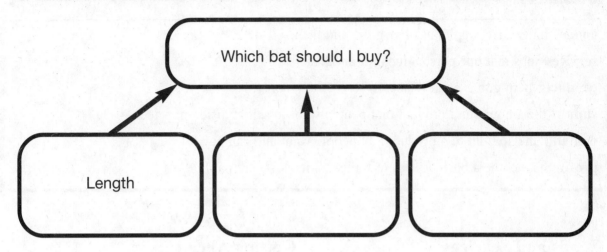

Which bat should I buy?

Length

2. Identify two examples of economic choices you have made. Tell what you picked and what you gave up.

_____

_____

_____

3. What is opportunity cost? Give an example.

_____

_____

_____

4. How did Robin's list help her make a choice?

_____

_____

_____

5. **Critical Thinking:** *Sequence* What steps did Robin follow as she made an economic choice to buy a bat?

_____

_____

_____

# Lesson 3: A Community Business

## Vocabulary

**goods**  things that people make or grow and then sell

**services**  jobs that one person does for another

**products**  both goods and services

**supply**  the amount of a product that people want to sell at different prices

**demand**  the amount of a product that people want and can pay for

**profit**  the income a business has left after all its costs are paid

## Goods and Services

Most communities have large businesses and small businesses. All businesses offer goods, services, or both. **Goods** are things people make or grow and then sell. Softball bats and vegetables are goods. **Services** are jobs that one person does for another. People who fix cars offer a service. **Products** are both goods and services.

## The Amount of a Product

Supply and demand can change the price of a product. **Supply** is the amount of a product that people want to sell. If supply goes up, prices usually go down. If a store has too many bats, the owner may lower the price of the bats. **Demand** is the amount of a product that people want and can pay for. If demand goes down, prices often go down. If few people want to buy bats, the store owner may lower the price of the bats.

## Getting Ahead

Businesses try to make a profit. A **profit** is the income a business has left over after all its costs are paid. Costs are things that a business spends money on. A business makes a profit only when it can sell a product for more than it costs to provide it. For example, owners of sporting goods stores try to buy bats from bat makers at the lowest possible price. The store owners make a profit by selling the bats for more money than they paid for the bats. Businesses can do things to increase, or raise, their profit. One thing businesses can do is to sell a product at a higher price. Businesses also can try to keep costs down.

# Lesson 3: Review

1. **Cause and Effect** Describe the different ways that prices of goods and services can change.

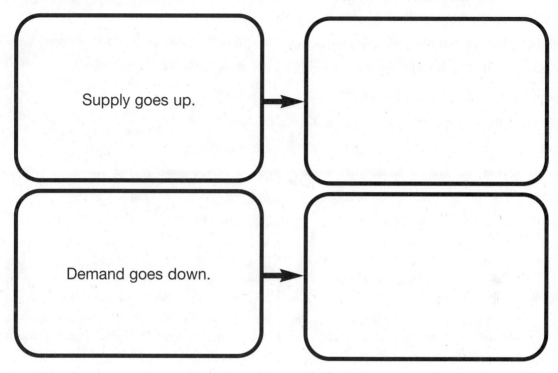

2. What are some examples of businesses that provide goods or services?

   _____

   _____

3. Would you expect the price of a valentine to be higher or lower after Valentine's Day? Why?

   _____

   _____

4. How can a business increase its profit?

   _____

   _____

5. **Critical Thinking: *Make Inferences*** If many farmers have a lot of tomatoes to sell, would you expect the price to be higher or lower? Why?

   _____

   _____

# Lesson 1: Using Resources

## Vocabulary

**renewable resource**  something taken from nature that can be replaced within a short time

**nonrenewable resource**  something taken from nature that cannot be replaced easily

**human resource**  a person who makes products or offers services

**producer**  a person who makes products

**specialize**  to do one job; to make one part of a product

**capital resource**  a machine, tool, or building used to make goods and services

## Using Natural Resources

Many goods are made from natural resources. Natural resources are things found in nature that people use. Trees and the wood that comes from them are renewable resources. A **renewable resource** can be replaced within a short time. A **nonrenewable resource** cannot be replaced easily. Coal, oil, and natural gas are nonrenewable resources. Inside factories, people and machines change renewable and nonrenewable resources into products. Workers in a softball bat factory make a piece of wood into a bat.

## People at Work

People work to change resources into goods. People who make products are called **human resources** or **producers.** Many of these people work in factories. Today factory workers mostly use machines to make products. Factory workers often **specialize** in one job. That means that a worker makes only one part of a product. Many specialized workers might help to make one product.

## Machines at Work

Machines, tools, and buildings are also used to make products. These things are called **capital resources.** Machines work faster than people. It used to take 15 minutes to cut and shape a bat by hand. Today machines can make one bat in about 15 seconds. Machines help make more products in less time. Now businesses can sell more bats at lower prices. This helps businesses make more money.

# Lesson 1: Review

1. **Sequence** Sequence the steps needed to make a softball bat.

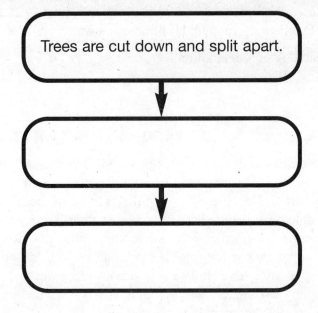

Trees are cut down and split apart.

2. How is a renewable resource different from a nonrenewable resource?

_____

_____

3. How do specialized workers help make goods?

_____

_____

4. How have machines changed the amount of time needed to cut and shape one bat?

_____

_____

5. **Critical Thinking:** *Cause and Effect* How can machines help a company make greater profits?

_____

_____

# Lesson 2: Depending on Others

## Vocabulary

**scarcity** not enough of something to meet all of people's wants and needs

**interdependence** depending on one another

## Too Few Resources

There are not enough resources to make everything people want or need. This means there is a **scarcity** of resources. Because resources are scarce, people must decide how to use them. For example, people must choose how to use wood. They might choose to build houses out of wood. People might also choose to use wood to make paper. Gasoline is another scarce resource. In 1941 many men were fighting in World War II. Because of this, male baseball players were scarce. To meet the demand for baseball, a women's league was formed in 1943. It was called the All-American Girls Professional Baseball League. Many people enjoyed women's baseball.

## Resources and Goods

Portland, Oregon, has many trees. People cut down the trees. Then they take the trees to a mill. At the mill the trees are made into boards called lumber. Truck drivers bring the lumber to communities that do not have many trees. Communities depend on one another for goods and resources. Depending on one another is known as **interdependence.**

## People Helping People

Land is another scarce resource. Communities must choose how they want to use their land. Communities need money in order to build on land. When money is scarce, people in a community depend on one another for help. Some people give money. Others offer goods and services. People in communities work together and share resources.

# Lesson 2: Review

1. 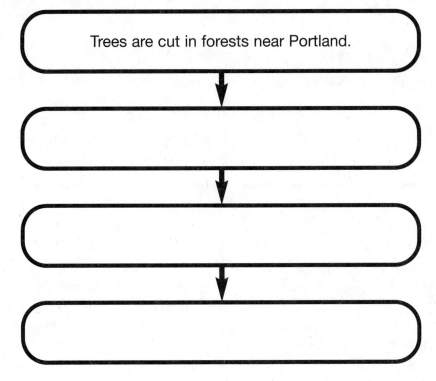 **Sequence** Sequence the path wood takes from forests near Portland to Phoenix.

Trees are cut in forests near Portland.

2. What are some scarce resources that people use?

_____

_____

3. How does wood get from the community where it is produced to the community where it is used?

_____

_____

4. How does scarcity cause people to depend on each other for goods and services?

_____

_____

5. **Critical Thinking:** *Cause and Effect* How did World War II lead to the formation of the All-American Girls Professional Baseball League?

_____

_____

# Lesson 3: A World of Trade

## Vocabulary

**trade** to buy or sell goods and services

**communication** the sharing of information or news

**international trade** trade between different countries

**import** to bring resources and other products from one country into another country

**export** to send resources and products to other countries

**free market** in a free market, people choose what to produce, sell, and buy

## Depending on Others

Communities all over the world **trade** with one another. They buy or sell goods and services from each other. Transportation makes trading possible. Airplanes, trains, ships, and trucks move goods from one part of the world to another very quickly. **Communication,** or the sharing of information, also helps countries trade with one another. A worker in a grocery store can use a phone or a computer to order more products.

## Trade Then and Now

People traded with one another long ago. People in one place usually made only a few kinds of goods. They would trade their goods with people from another place. For example, people in ancient Greece traded with people in Egypt. Greeks made pottery. They traded pottery for goods they needed, such as wheat. Greeks used wheat to make bread. People in ancient Rome also traded with people in Egypt. Romans traded crops for silk cloth. They used the cloth to make clothing. Today people usually trade goods and services for money. One person uses money to buy a product from another. People trade with each other because trading is helpful to both of them.

## Trade Between Countries

People all over the world trade with one another. Trade between different countries is called **international trade.** People import products. **Import** means to bring resources or products from one country into another country. People also export products. **Export** means to send products to other countries.

## Free Markets

The United States has a **free market.** In a free market, people can decide what they want to make. They also can choose what they want to buy. Farmers may choose which vegetables to grow. People then can choose which vegetables to buy. Some countries do not have a free market. Their governments decide what people can buy and sell.

# Lesson 3: Review

1. **Compare and Contrast** Compare and contrast trade long ago with trade now.

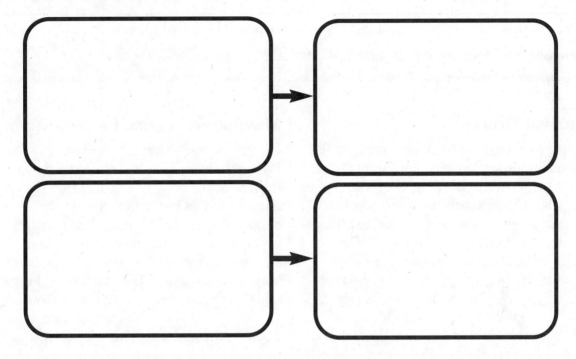

2. How have modern transportation and communication changed trade?

_____

_____

3. What is the reason people choose to trade?

_____

_____

4. How did people in ancient Greece and Rome use the goods for which they traded?

_____

_____

5. **Critical Thinking:** *Fact and Opinion* Which of the following are statements of fact, and
   which are statements of opinion?
   **a.** World trade has made the world a better place.
   **b.** The United States has a free market.
   **c.** In a free market, people and companies decide what is bought and sold.

_____

_____

# Lesson 1: Governments in the Past

## Vocabulary

**direct democracy** a government that is run by the people who live under it

**republic** a government in which citizens elect other people to speak for them

## Ancient Greece

People long ago formed communities for the same reasons we do today. They wanted a safe place to live, work, and play. They also wanted fair laws. Citizens made laws in ancient Athens, a city in Greece. Citizens are official members of a community or nation. The government in Athens was called a **direct democracy.** In a direct democracy, citizens run the government. In the United States today, our government is a **republic.** In a republic, citizens elect people to speak for them. These people are called representatives. In 1215 King John of England signed a paper. The paper was called the Magna Carta. It said that the king had to follow the law. He also had to ask citizens before he made decisions.

## Mayflower Compact

In 1620 colonists from England came to Plymouth, Massachusetts. They sailed on a ship called the *Mayflower*. The colonists left England so that they could practice their religion the way they wanted. Their leaders wrote a plan of government to make laws for the community. The plan was called the Mayflower Compact. The Mayflower Compact said that the colonists would make laws for their community. Everyone in the community would follow the laws. This was the first time European colonists came up with a plan to make laws for themselves. The founders of the United States used the Mayflower Compact as an example to follow later.

# Lesson 1: Review

1. 🔄 **Summarize** Fill in details that support the lesson summary.

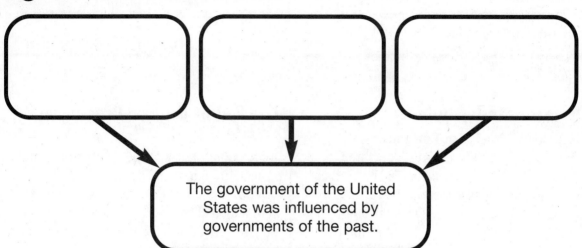

2. Why do people form communities?

_____

_____

_____

3. Why did the English colonists create a plan of government?

_____

_____

_____

4. Why was the Mayflower Compact an important plan?

_____

_____

_____

5. **Critical Thinking:** *Draw Conclusions* Why do you think that the Magna Carta was an important document?

_____

_____

_____

# Lesson 2: United States Government

## Vocabulary

**amendment**  a change

## Declaring Independence

Many colonists felt that England was taking away their rights. The colonists declared, or announced, their independence from England. Independence means freedom. Thomas Jefferson helped write the Declaration of Independence in 1776. The Declaration of Independence has three parts. The first part says that people have rights. These rights are the right to life, the right to be free, and the right to try to build a happy life for themselves. The government must protect these rights. The second part lists the ways the king of England took away the colonists' rights. The third part said that the colonies were no longer part of England.

## The U.S. Constitution

The U.S. Constitution was written in 1787. The U.S. Constitution is a plan for the government of the United States. Many people worked to write this plan. George Washington was the leader of the group who wrote it. Benjamin Franklin and James Madison also helped write the Constitution. The Constitution gave the people, not a king, the right to rule.

## The Bill of Rights: Protecting Freedom

Some people felt that the Constitution did not protect enough of their rights. In 1791 ten **amendments,** or changes, to the Constitution were added. These ten amendments are called the Bill of Rights. The Bill of Rights protects some rights of the people. Some of these rights are freedom of speech, freedom of religion, and the right to gather together. African Americans sometimes were treated differently than other Americans. Rosa Parks tried to change this in the 1950s. Other African Americans joined her work to protect their rights. Laws were finally passed to protect all people's rights. Thurgood Marshall was the first African American judge on the United States Supreme Court. He worked to make sure that all people's rights were protected.

Use with pages 366–371.

# Lesson 2: Review

1. ↻ **Summarize** Fill in details to complete the lesson summary.

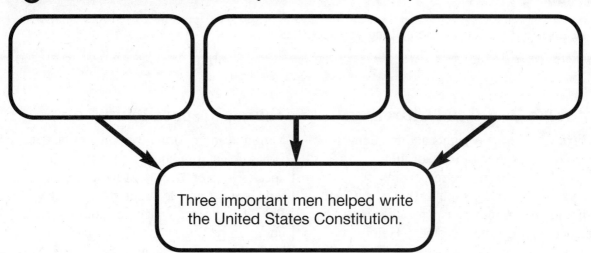

Three important men helped write
the United States Constitution.

2. What three rights does the Declaration of Independence say that people have?

_____

_____

_____

3. Why was the Bill of Rights added to the Constitution?

_____

_____

_____

4. How did Rosa Parks's community change because of her actions?

_____

_____

_____

5. **Critical Thinking:** *Compare and Contrast* How are the Declaration of Independence and the Bill of Rights alike and different?

_____

_____

_____

# Lesson 3: Being a Good Citizen

## Vocabulary

**responsibility** a duty, or something you should do

## Ways to Be a Good Citizen

Citizens have many rights and freedoms. They also have **responsibilities,** or things they should do. Citizens are responsible for obeying laws. They should pay taxes. Citizens should vote. Another responsibility is respecting the rights of others. Helping to make the community a better place is also a responsibility.

## Taking Responsibility

Voting is an important responsibility. Citizens vote to elect, or choose, leaders. Leaders speak for us on important issues. Americans vote to elect people to run their country. People also elect leaders to run their state and community. Before they vote, people listen to the leaders who want to be elected. Next, they decide who they think would do the best job. Finally, they vote. Working to make the community better is another important responsibility. People can make their community a better place by volunteering to help others. When people volunteer, they are not paid. They help others because they want to. People might volunteer to help people who are hungry or need clothing.

Name _____ Date _____

# Lesson 3: Review

1. 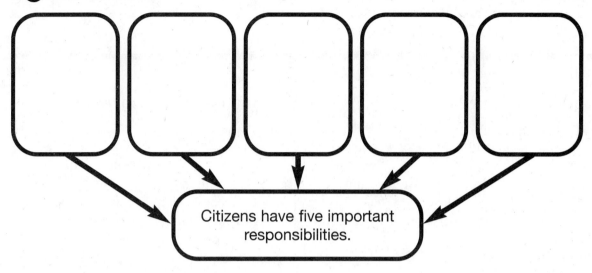 **Summarize** Fill in the details to complete the summary of this lesson.

Citizens have five important responsibilities.

2. What is a responsibility?

_____

_____

_____

3. Who speaks for the people of the United States on important issues?

_____

_____

_____

4. What is one way to help improve your community?

_____

_____

_____

5. **Critical Thinking:** *Sequence* What are three steps in voting for leaders?

_____

_____

_____

# Lesson 1: Community Services

## Vocabulary

**recreation**  a way of enjoying yourself

## Services People Want

People in communities want services that offer them safety, education, transportation, and **recreation.** Recreation is a way of enjoying yourself. Local, or community, governments offer these services. The services help make the community a good place to live.

## Services Local Governments Provide

Police and fire departments are services that offer people safety. They protect people. Schools are services that give people an education. People also can read books at libraries. Recreation is also important to people. Many communities have parks where people can play sports. Some communities have swimming pools. Local governments also offer transportation services. They fix and build roads. Some governments run buses and trains. It costs money for local governments to offer services. The people in your community pay for them.

## Paying for Local Government

The local government gets money to pay for services in three ways. First, people pay taxes to their local government. The local government uses these taxes to pay for services people want. Second, the local government might charge people money for some services. For example, you might have to pay to swim in your community pool. Third, the local government gets money from the state and United States government.

# Lesson 1: Review

1. 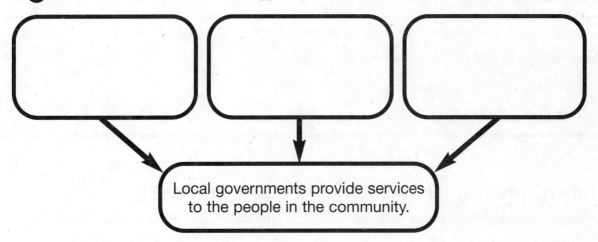 **Summarize** Fill in details that support the lesson summary.

Local governments provide services to the people in the community.

2. Why do local governments provide services the people want?

_____

_____

_____

3. What services help meet a community's need for safety and security?

_____

_____

_____

4. Name one way that local governments get money for the services that they provide.

_____

_____

_____

5. **Critical Thinking:** *Summarize* Identify the four types of services usually provided by local governments.

_____

_____

_____

# Lesson 2: Community Leaders

## Vocabulary

**council** a group of people who make laws and rules for a community

**mayor** a leader of a community

**candidate** a person who runs for office

**consent** permission

## Government Officials

Adults in your community vote for local leaders. They elect, or choose, a town or city **council.** A council is a group of people who make laws for a community. Adults may also elect a **mayor.** The mayor leads the community. Sometimes the council chooses the mayor. The mayor and the council run the local government. They choose people to do certain jobs, such as the police chief. The park district board makes most decisions about parks and recreation activities. The citizens usually elect the members of the park district board. The school board makes rules for the community's schools. The citizens elect the members of the school board. The superintendent of schools carries out rules made by the school board. The school board usually picks the superintendent.

## Electing Leaders

**Candidates** are people who are running for office. Candidates talk to people in the community. Candidates explain how they will help the community. The people listen. Next, they compare what different candidates have said. Finally, people vote for the person they think will do the best job.

## Consent of the People

People want their leaders to make and carry out laws. People give their **consent,** or permission, to leaders to do this. People agree to follow the laws. If leaders do not do a good job, people will not vote for them again. The leaders will no longer have the power to speak for the people.

# Lesson 2: Review

1. 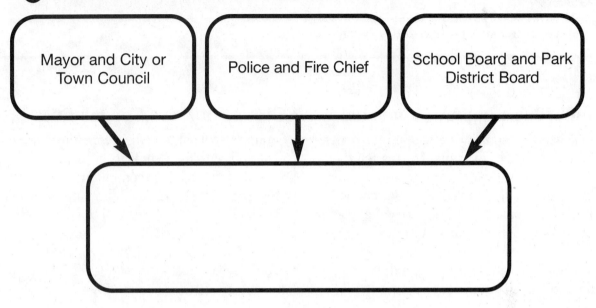 **Summarize** Fill in a sentence to summarize this lesson.

2. Identify six local officials and explain how they are chosen.

_____

_____

3. What happens if a leader does not do a good job?

_____

_____

4. Whose job is it to carry out the rules made by the school board?

_____

_____

5. **Critical Thinking:** *Compare and Contrast* How is government as described in this lesson the same or different from your local government?

_____

_____

# Lesson 3: People Change Communities

## Vocabulary

**marsh** an area of land sometimes covered by water

## Individuals Improve Communities

One person can make a community a better place to live. For example, Martha felt that it was not safe for people to ride their bikes on busy streets. She wanted her city to build bike lanes for people to ride in. She wrote a letter to the city council. She asked other people to write letters to the city council. Because of Martha, bike lanes are being built in cities around the country.

## Groups Improve Communities

Groups also can make their community a better place to live. Students at Silver Bay School improved their community. They noticed that there was trash in the **marsh** near the Toms River. They decided to clean up the marsh. They also asked other people to clean up areas near the river. It worked. Other people began cleaning up the river. The students made their community a better place.

# Lesson 3: Review

1. ⟳ **Summarize** Fill in details to complete the lesson summary.

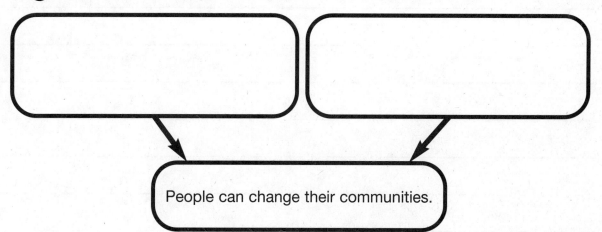

People can change their communities.

2. What is one way that people can try to change their community?

_____

_____

_____

3. What decision did a group of students make?

_____

_____

_____

4. How did Silver Bay School students change their community?

_____

_____

_____

5. **Critical Thinking:** *Cause and Effect* The students from Toms River saw that the marsh was littered. What effect did the students' actions have on the marsh?

_____

_____

_____

# NOTES

# NOTES

# NOTES

# NOTES

# NOTES

# NOTES

# NOTES

# NOTES

# NOTES

# NOTES

# NOTES

# NOTES

# NOTES

# NOTES

# NOTES